A Beautiful Exchange

A Thirty-Day Devotional
for Women Featuring the
Best Things in Life

DESTINY K. SUAREZ

WESTBOW
PRESS®
A DIVISION OF THOMAS NELSON
& ZONDERVAN

WestBow Press books may be ordered through booksellers or by contacting:

WestBow Press
A Division of Thomas Nelson & Zondervan
1663 Liberty Drive
Bloomington, IN 47403
www.westbowpress.com
844-714-3454

Because of the dynamic nature of the Internet, any web addresses or links contained in this book may have changed since publication and may no longer be valid. The views expressed in this work are solely those of the author and do not necessarily reflect the views of the publisher, and the publisher hereby disclaims any responsibility for them.

Any people depicted in stock imagery provided by Getty Images are models, and such images are being used for illustrative purposes only. Certain stock imagery © Getty Images.

Scripture marked (NKJV) taken from the New King James Version®. Copyright © 1982 by Thomas Nelson. Used by permission. All rights reserved.

Scripture marked (KJV) taken from the King James Version of the Bible.

ISBN: 978-1-6642-1554-2 (sc)
ISBN: 978-1-6642-1556-6 (hc)
ISBN: 978-1-6642-1555-9 (e)

Library of Congress Control Number: 2020924089

Print information available on the last page.

WestBow Press rev. date: 02/01/2021

Presented To:

_____

From:

_____

Date:

_____

Contents

Acknowledgments

I have been surrounded by remarkable and highly inspiring people in my life.

Keith Suarez: Thank you for choosing me to be your wife. I love your presence by my side and your constant encouragement to pursue my dreams. It makes me love you even more.

Julie Kirby: Thank you for always supporting me, giving me advice, and reminding me that if I follow God's lead, I will never fail. I love knowing you wanted to be the first to have a copy of my book.

Janice Kirby: Thank you for being my Naomi and taking me to church every Sunday. Thank you for trusting God's lead, which caused me to follow also.

Larry and Marsha Plyer: I'm so thankful to have you both as pastor and children's ministry director for much of my childhood. You hold such a special place in my heart. I'll never forget the Sunday night I gave my heart to Jesus during Team Kids.

Mrs. Elizabeth Yarbrough, Mrs. Lynn Babb, Mrs. Linda Tucker, Mrs. Lisa Faulks, Ms. Mae Williams, Mrs. Wanda Bright, Mrs. Janice Smith, and Ms. Cheryl Smith: Thank you for being my Sunday school teachers. Thank you for pouring God's Word into my heart week after week. You taught me how to love and gave me the desire to go into ministry.

Ricky and Sheila Cook: I'm so glad God sent us to your church. Thank you, Ricky, for giving me my first opportunity to minister. You both have truly invested in my life, and for that I am so grateful.

Cathy Fitzgerald: Thank you for being my right-hand lady throughout my entire journey of becoming a published author. You have an eye and gift for editing. I appreciate having you in my life and all you have done for me.

Angie Raymond: Thank you for always encouraging me to continue writing. You are a gem.

Destiny K. Suarez

Hold Me Now

Lord help me.
Take me back
Where I can rest in Your peace.

Heal my heart, make me whole.
Fill this emptiness;
Restore my soul

Reach for my hand,
Hold me close—
Sweet release
In the shelter of Your wings.

Calm the storm;
Surround me
With gentleness. I need You now;
I love You still.

Through the madness
There's no disguise.
I know You're watching.
Hold me now.

I've come so far.
I've learned to stand
As You hold my hand,
Never letting go.

You are my Lord,
The Redeemer of my soul.
Hold me now.

—Destiny K. Suarez

Broken?

I will praise You, for I am fearfully and wonderfully
made;
Marvelous are Your works,
And that my soul knows very well.

—Psalm 139:14

Ugly. Unwelcome. Unwanted. Unloved.

Do these words bring back shuddering thoughts that have been
spoken over you, or do you recall using these words to define yourself
as you've looked in the mirror? I once heard that if we talked to
others the way we talk to ourselves, we wouldn't have any friends at
all. I chuckle as I'm reminded of this quote because I know it's been
true in my life.

We sometimes talk to ourselves in ways that we would never talk
to our friends or even possibly our worst enemies. We label ourselves
and let these labels define us. If we've been called a name, that
name is cemented in our minds. If we've been rejected, we classify
ourselves as unwanted. A traumatic time can define us as broken

for months and years afterward. There is no doubt we must walk through and face these daunting words and experiences in life until we find healing, but it's not a place to stay forever.

Just because it was said or thought doesn't mean it's true. Just imagine for a moment that the words spoken over us, or that we've spoken about ourselves, are written on sticky notes and taped to our shirts. We all know how easily that tape will pull away from the cotton and eventually fall to the floor. It will likely fall without our noticing. This is what we need to do with untrue words. It's time to pull the labels off. After all, they were never superglued to us. These words will only stick as long as we allow them to.

How often do we put a label on ourselves that is extinguished through God's grace? With His grace we can peel off all the doubts, the areas where we fall short, and the hateful words spoken about us. By His redemptive power, He can rescue us and heal our hearts and minds. He reminds us in His Word to "bring every thought into captivity."[1] Every time those words come to mind, we are to reject them and remind ourselves of the truth. Oh, how beautiful is His truth about us in Ephesians 1. We are blessed, chosen, adopted, favored, redeemed, and forgiven. We are children of God. Choose today to cling to His truth: You are fearfully and wonderfully made.

Thoughts and reflections:

_____

_____

_____

_____

_____

_____

_____

---

[1] 2 Corinthians 10:5

Destiny K. Suarez

Best Thing in Life:

Flipping your pillow over to the cold side.

What's Your Name?

For You formed my inward parts;
You covered me in my mother's womb.
I will praise You, for I am fearfully and wonderfully
made;
Marvelous are Your works,
And that my soul knows very well.
—Psalm 139:13–14

Have you ever noticed there are many women in the Bible who are not mentioned by name? We only know their stories of distress, sin, and need for a savior.

One example is the woman at the well in John 4. Every day she went to the well alone to get some water. Another is the woman with the issue of blood in Matthew 9:20–22. She had spent every day for the last twelve years bleeding to death, going from one doctor to another, only to be left financially broke and publicly shunned. Each woman had a story, but there is never a mention of their names in scripture.

The one thing these two women had in common was an

encounter with Jesus that changed their lives. Jesus recognized the faith the woman with the issue of blood had, without her ever disclosing herself to Him. The woman at the well had secrets—five husbands and a live-in boyfriend. Jesus knew all about her life story but was more concerned with her soul. He knew He could give her His living water, and she would never be spiritually thirsty again.

Can you relate to these women? Have you been labeled by what you've done or what's been done to you, as if these things are what define you instead of who you really are?

God has been God for a very long time—forever, actually. One day God decided He wanted to make you. He knew exactly who you would become, what would fuel your fire, and what you would be sensitive to. Before you were born, He knew you. After imagining you, He created you. He knit you in your mother's womb.

This brings to mind my dear Nanny. She sewed Easter dresses and church dresses for my sister and me. She even made my first formal dress. First, an idea would come, and then she purchased the cloth and pattern and thread to match perfectly. She was so good with her sewing machine that she could take a roll of thread and a sheet of material and create the most beautiful dresses ever seen.

God does the same with us. He forms us from the dust of the earth. He knows more than just our stories; He knows our inmost beings. He knows the deepest places of our hearts and every hair on our heads. He knows our names.

I love the beautiful song David wrote revealing God's deepest love for us in Psalm 139:

> O Lord, You have searched me and known me.
> You know my sitting down and my rising up;
> You understand my thought afar off.
> You comprehend my path and my lying down,
> And are acquainted with all my ways.
> For there is not a word on my tongue,
> But behold, O Lord, You know it altogether.

You have hedged me behind and before,
And laid Your hand upon me.
Such knowledge is too wonderful for me;
It is high, I cannot attain it.[2]

For You formed my inward parts;
You covered me in my mother's womb.
I will praise You, for I am fearfully and wonderfully
made;
Marvelous are Your works,
And that my soul knows very well.
My frame was not hidden from You,
When I was made in secret,
And skillfully wrought in the lowest parts of the earth.
Your eyes saw my substance, being yet unformed.
And in Your book they all were written,
The days fashioned for me,
When as yet there were none of them.[3]

Thoughts and reflections:

_____

_____

_____

_____

_____

_____

_____

---

[2] Psalm 139:1–6
[3] Psalm 139:13–16

Destiny K. Suarez

Best Thing in Life:

Getting a warm towel from the dryer to dry off with.

Unfinished

And the vessel that he made of clay was marred in the hand of the potter; so he made it again into another vessel, as it seemed good to the potter to make.

—Jeremiah 18:4

But now, O Lord,
You are our Father;
We are the clay, and You are our potter;
And all we are the work of Your hand.

—Isaiah 64:8

Portraits are paint, and pottery is clay. Without the main element, a masterpiece cannot be created. Leonardo da Vinci's *Mona Lisa* began as a blank canvas with many colors of paint on a palette. A brush of paint here and detail there eventually led to the creation of this well-known portrait. The same goes with pottery. It first begins as dirt from the earth, and when mixed with water, it becomes clay.

Destiny K. Suarez

The potter can form the clay into any shape he or she wishes and seal his or her creation with heat or by leaving it out to dry completely. Do you remember playing with plastic teacups as a little girl? I remember rushing to the bathroom and using cold water that would magically turn to tea or sneaking to the kitchen to use my leftover fruit punch from dinner for my tea parties. Plastic teacups are like fine china to a little girl.

As I got older, I became mesmerized by porcelain. It's so fragile and dainty and usually reserved for special occasions. One day while I was cleaning my porcelain teacup to prepare for a party, the handle broke, and so did my heart. The sentimental value was so great I couldn't bear the thought of throwing it away, so I decided to use it as my new tasting bowl when I would make dinner.

From start to finish, we have a lot in common with a teacup. Before a potter begins to mold the clay, he or she has an idea in mind of what he or she will make. We're envisioned by God before ever conceived. Our mothers and fathers are the elements that bring us to life. When we're born, we have no reputation other than who our family is. As we get older, we discover our likes and dislikes, what makes our tempers flare, and what soothes our souls. We become worn from life's attacks yet are comforted by dear friends in times of loss. We chase dreams and find that some of them weren't meant for us. We grow strong in our faith and win many spiritual victories; other times we feel like Israelites faced with Goliath.

Doubt, failure, and frustration can leave us feeling like broken creations. Disappointed in ourselves, we wonder if it's time to rip the canvas or shatter the clay. We believe we should be farther along in our walks with the Lord than we are. Just as the potter doesn't throw away the clay when it bubbles or cracks, God doesn't dispose of us either. He molds and remakes us with His love and grace.

Our potter, God, wants us to know He has begun a good work in us and will be faithful to complete it.[4] We're on a journey with

---

[4] Philippians 1:6

God. On mountaintops, He celebrates with us, and in the valley, He holds us close. He makes beauty from ashes[5] and promises to make everything work together for our good.[6] The beating of our hearts reminds us there's a purpose and plan for us here on earth.

God doesn't see us as damaged goods when we fall short. We're masterpieces—just unfinished.

Thoughts and reflections:

_____

_____

_____

_____

_____

_____

_____

---

[5] Isaiah 61:3
[6] Romans 8:28

Destiny K. Suarez

Best Thing in Life:

Coming inside to air-conditioning after being in the heat.

To Just Be

And do not be conformed to this world, but be transformed by the renewing of your mind, that you may prove what is that good and acceptable and perfect will of God.

—Romans 12:2

Have you ever lain awake in the dead of night wondering what your life should be or what could have been? Feeling lost and alone? Reflecting on the life you have now compared to what you envisioned? Questioning whether you're doing what you're supposed to do?

The world has many ways of pulling us toward new desires. It reminds me of the old saying, "Keeping up with the Joneses." We pray for a godly husband and a family of our own. When God answers our prayers, we're overjoyed; however, sometimes this feeling is temporary. Once we see someone with a four-bedroom home and we only have two bedrooms, we begin to feel discontent.

Living in a social networking world, it's easy to compare ourselves with others. Recently, I developed a fetish for a new popular watch.

It receives text alerts and has GPS, calendar reminders, the internet, and more, all without needing to carry your phone. While shopping, I found myself in the entertainment section, comparing prices to see which watch version would be best.

After leaving the store, I had a revelation. I don't ever wear a watch. Why would I pay two hundred dollars or more for something I don't wear in the first place? I realized I wanted it solely because I lacked it. It seemed everyone around me had one. I didn't need it and honestly didn't want it. Yes, the features were amazing, but it just wasn't "me."

Chasing this world leaves us empty. Is it wrong to buy things we like or to have dreams for the future? No, unless it causes us to measure our lives against others, to anxiously search for more, and to eagerly anticipate the next moment instead of basking in the present. A dear friend once told me, "When we feel restless, it's because we have been spending more time with the world than with our Lord." When we feel unsettled and dissatisfied, we need to come back to the throne room of grace, into God's presence, and spend some time with Him in prayer. God will transform and renew our minds to a state of contentment.

Lord, help us rest and find the beauty in the season we're in. Help us not to be stressed, but to be content. To find rest and solitude. To stop wishing and wondering. To just be and embrace today.

Thoughts and reflections:

_____

_____

_____

_____

_____

_____

_____

Best Thing in Life:

Fresh linens on your bed.

Walking by Faith

A man's heart plans his way,
But the Lord directs his steps.

—Proverbs 16:9

Your word is a lamp to my feet,
And a light to my path.

—Psalm 119:105

Wouldn't it be convenient if we could put our current life status in a GPS that would tell us exactly what we should do? A navigation system is good to have when we're lost in the car, but it doesn't give us much help when it comes to making decisions about our personal lives.

Recently, I had a series of events happen that were not favorable. After I'd replayed scenarios in my head, my heart reminded me that God isn't surprised by this. He isn't panicking about the situation, and He already knows how it will work out, even before I was born.[7]

---

[7] Jeremiah 1:5

I'm not the author of my life, and it isn't up to me to figure life out. I can take solace and peace in the truth of God's Word. How vast, how great, and how true it is.

When you feel you've lost your way, remember, God doesn't give you a map explaining the complete route of your life. He gives you a compass. As you trust Him and seek Him in every area of your life, He will order your steps, bringing light to the next revelation, the next answer, or the next route.

We aren't given every turn, every stop, and every detour of our lives from beginning to end. We are given God's Word, the Bible, to guide us. It is full of His promises, truths, faithfulness, love, and reminders of His covenant: "I work all things for the good of those who love me."[8]

We can rest in knowing that, when we put our complete trust in God, He will guide us from our current location to our next destination, whether it's finding a new job, looking for a new home, handling a marital dispute, or asking for wisdom in raising children. His Word will be a lamp that lights up the darkness and a guiding light to our path.

Thoughts and reflections:

_____

_____

_____

_____

_____

_____

_____

---

[8] Romans 8:28, paraphrased

Best Thing in Life:

Taking your hair down from a ponytail after a long day.

A Long-Distance Call Home

Be anxious for nothing, but in everything by prayer and supplication, with thanksgiving, let your requests be made known to God.

—Philippians 4:6

Come to Me, all you who labor and are heavy laden, and I will give you rest. Take My yoke upon you and learn from Me, for I am gentle and lowly in heart, and you will find rest for your souls. For My yoke is easy and My burden is light.

—Matthew 11:28–30

Where will I get the money for my next rent payment? How will I work full-time and pay for day care for my son? How will I reconcile the dispute with my mother-in-law, who doesn't see what she has said as wrong? How will I talk to my boss about a situation that seems immoral to me? I need to go to the gym, wash dishes, fold four loads of laundry, mop the kitchen, get Anna to her dance recital, and put dinner in the Crock-Pot, all by 1:00 p.m. today. How will I ever get it all done?

Are you as tired as I am after reading this list? We were never meant to carry the load and "do life" on our own. God doesn't want us to be anxious about *anything*. Not one thing. This concept is hard to comprehend when we're trying to stay afloat in our own circumstances. Therefore, He tells us to come to Him. He knows how overwhelming life can be for us. He wants us to bring our to-do list, worries, and fears to Him. He's literally telling us to take it off our backs, throw it all at His feet, and put on His peace. But how?

Prayer is our outlet. It's our long-distance call home to our Father. He's so good. He wants us to come to Him in prayer and bring everything to Him: the good, the bad, and the ugly, the easy stuff and the hard stuff. He wants to carry us when we're weary. He wants to pull us from life's raging waters and let us rest by still waters. He wants to restore our souls[9] from the busyness of the world and the expectations of those around us, rescue us from the chaos, and give us His yoke.

Jesus' yoke is His way of balancing and doing life. His way is light. It's easy. It's comforting. In Bible times a yoke was used to bind oxen together to carry a load. Jesus wants us to come and latch up beside him so He can carry our load.

Next time you feel overwhelmed, go to Him in prayer, giving Him everything that is unsettling you. He will pour His peace into you and help you balance every area of your life.

---

[9] Psalm 23:3

Thoughts and reflections:

_____

_____

_____

_____

_____

_____

_____

Best Thing in Life:

Sight of fresh cut grass.

Bathed in His Love

Therefore, having these promises, beloved, let us cleanse ourselves from all filthiness of the flesh and spirit, perfecting holiness in the fear of God.

—2 Corinthians 7:1

If we confess our sins, He is faithful and just to forgive us our sins and to cleanse us from all unrighteousness.

—1 John 1:9

Does your car stay shiny for more than a day? Not mine! When you live in the South, pollen is like a blanket to cars in the spring, and my gravel driveway adds a coat of gray dust overtop the silver sparkle of my car. Now let's not talk about the inside of the car and how quickly it needs to be vacuumed out, especially after my shoes bring in grass and dirt following a rainstorm.

Though a dirty car isn't something I pride myself in, I must admit I love having my car washed, especially when I get a free car wash coupon after having my car serviced. I love driving slowly into the car wash as I hear the water spray my tires and undercarriage. I drive in until I'm signaled to stop, put the car in park, and relax. The pipes spray water on both sides of my car until the entire surface is saturated with water. Then comes my favorite part, the bubbly soap. The colorful soap sprays my car until it's covered like a toddler in a bubble bath. I thoroughly enjoy watching the soap run together on my windshield breaking down the dirt. Next, I watch the water spray vehemently out of the pipes and wash all the dirt and soap away.

Just as the car wash cleans our cars, saturating ourselves in God's love cleanses all the sin and unrighteousness in our heart. When Jesus died for our sins, His blood forgave all sins. He died a horrific death to show us how much He loved us so we would get to live in heaven with Him.

Prior to Jesus' death, He washed His disciples' feet. As He washed their feet, He demonstrated what love looks like. I'm sure their feet were smelly and extremely dirty, since they walked down dusty roads, in sandals, everywhere they went.

As He poured water into a basin and humbly washed their feet, He made them physically clean. In addition, He emotionally cleansed the disciples by becoming a servant to them even though He was their Master. Jesus washed all His disciples' feet even though one of them, Judas, would soon betray Him.

The next day Jesus would be beaten until He was unrecognizable[10] and would die on a cross for our sins. He did this so we would be forgiven for every wrong thought, motive, or action. He knew we needed a Savior, and only the shedding of His blood would be enough to forgive our sins. Because of the love and sacrifice of His own life, we can confess our sins by being bathed in His love, be scrubbed clean from the filthiness of our sins, and be white as snow.[11]

---

[10] Isaiah 52:14
[11] Isaiah 1:18

Thoughts and reflections:

_____

_____

_____

_____

_____

_____

_____

Best Thing in Life:

The first spoonful of peanut butter from a new jar.

I Steer Where I Stare

You will seek me and find me, when you seek me
with all your heart.

—Jeremiah 29:13

If you're like me, you have a to-do list in the Memo Pad of your
phone, as well as other pages titled "Things to Buy," "Goals," "Gift
Ideas," and so on. Let's not forget the calendar alarm reminders.
Honestly, I have so many lists because my brain cannot recall all the
details of everything I need to remember.

If I dig deeper within myself, I realize there's more to this
phenomenon than just possible forgetfulness; think fear of failure.
Sometimes my to-do list overwhelms me. It seems the to-dos
never end. I'll delete two completed tasks, then add three more
commitments. It all just leaves me tired. I'm sure you're tired too.

It reminds me of the story of Mary and Martha. Martha invited
Jesus to her home while busily making sure the home smelled "fresh
as linen." She probably brought out the bleach cleaner of Bible days
to make sure all counters were disinfected, all the pillows fluffed on
the couches, and every crumb on the floor swept away.

Her sister, Mary, communed with Jesus. She gave Him her full attention and wasn't distracted by anything else. As Martha watched Mary, she became so frustrated that she questioned Jesus about her sister's behavior: "Lord, don't you care that my sister has left me to do the work by myself? Therefore, tell her to help me!"[12] I'm sure we can all agree that Martha was hoping that Jesus would suggest that Mary help, but that was not at all how Jesus answered. Jesus responded to Martha's plea by saying, "Martha, Martha, you are worried and troubled about many things, but one things is needed—indeed. Mary has chosen that good part, which will not be taken away from her."[13]

Jesus' response brought awareness to Martha about her priorities, which were taking her attention away from the one thing she truly needed most—time spent with the Lord. The household chores were of measly importance compared to spending time with the Messiah. Although we have obligations, we need (as she did) to evaluate their place and not allow them to consume us.

Living in our modern world, we can find our schedules fully packed where there isn't much time left to spend with God. We are pressured to perform by having the immaculate home with updated appliances, kids who make the honor roll and get into the best universities, and gourmet meals at the dinner table every night, all while maintaining the appearance of a trophy wife. This fantasy doesn't include tantrums, messy spills, oversleeping for work, or forgetting to make cookies for the school's bake sale. This world can leave us tired and unfulfilled—like Martha.

What our minds steadily think about and where we stare is the direction our day is steered. We can't let unrealistic pressures and demanding schedules define what is most important. Let us seek Jesus first in the morning with our whole hearts, giving our day to

---

12 Luke 10:40
13 Luke 10:41–42

Him. He will direct our steps.[14] When we rest in Him, the noise of the world and the chaos of to-do lists will fade. In His presence, you can cultivate peace and draw closer to Him.

Thoughts and reflections:

_____

_____

_____

_____

_____

_____

_____

Best Thing in Life:

Taking off your bra.

Planted, Not Buried

For he shall be like a tree planted by the waters,
Which spreads out its roots by the river,
And will not fear when heat comes;
But its leaf will be green,
And will not be anxious in the year of drought,
Nor will cease from yielding fruit.

—Jeremiah 17:8

Recently I tried on an adorable dress, only to realize once I put my arms through the sleeves and pulled it down over my bust that it was too small. I began mentally panicking as if I'd never be able to take the dress off: *Please don't rip. Please come off. What was I thinking? Will I ever get out of this dress?* After tugging one side a little and then the other back and forth for what felt like twenty minutes, I was finally able to wiggle myself out.

On the way home, I thought about how my dressing room experience imitates difficult seasons in life. Similar questions arise when I'm feeling disappointed, fearful, and helpless. *How long will this last? This is uncomfortable. Am I going to mess something up? Will I be able to get out of this thing? When will it be over?* The weight of life feels stronger than we are, and we're ready for difficult circumstances to end and to be restored. We feel as though we've been buried in our distress, yet what if perhaps we've been planted?

In the heat of life's battles, this is an incomprehensible thought, but let it soak into your heart: you are planted, not buried. Remember the story of Esther? She was chosen to be queen prior to the king plotting to destroy and kill the Jews, her family's lineage.

Her uncle Mordecai was troubled when he heard about the king's motives and told Esther, "Yet who knows whether you have come to the kingdom for such a time as this?"[15] His faith knew the title she held could change her family's future. This was a heavy request of Esther. Her asking for the Jews' lives to be spared would require her to risk life itself to enter the king's presence uninvited.

Just like Esther, you're a seed intentionally planted by God, not to be buried in the ground to be discarded but to thrive and bloom. The place you have been planted, your job, the family you were born into, the team your children play on, and the neighborhood you live in all have significance for this moment in time. You are cast in a role only you can live.

Let your roots be saturated in God's presence, knowing He is with you even in the drought. With Him, you will never cease yielding fruit, and your seed will become a great harvest. After all, you've been created for such a time as this.

Thoughts and reflections:

_____

_____

_____

_____

_____

_____

_____

---

[15] Esther 4:14

Best Thing in Life:

The first bite of homemade cobbler, fresh from the oven, with a scoop of vanilla ice cream on top.

Pressing Pause

Remember the Sabbath day, to keep it holy. Six
days you shall labor and do all your work, but the
seventh day is the Sabbath of the Lord your God. In
it you shall do no work: you, nor your son, nor your
daughter, nor your male servant, nor your female
servant, nor your cattle, nor your stranger who is
within your gates. For in six days the Lord made
the heavens and the earth, the sea, and all that is
in them, and rested the seventh day. Therefore the
Lord blessed the Sabbath day and hallowed it.

—Exodus 20:8–11

A year or so ago, the Lord began convicting me about Sundays—
about it being a day of rest. I wanted to honor His command, but I
really didn't know how. For eleven years, I was in full-time ministry
out of town, anywhere between forty-five minutes and over an
hour away. A lot of times I found myself working extra on Sundays,
because I loved what I did, so much that I could be content living
at the church.

After getting married and having a baby and a home to take care of, along with ministry, resting on Sunday became a juggling match for me. How was resting possible? During that time, a friend advised me to pick another day of the week to be my Sabbath day. I wasn't trying to be difficult, but I didn't see how I could make it work.

Fast-forward to now. I currently serve in church but not in a position of leadership during services. I'm a mom and a wife who works from home, and I attend church services regularly. It should be easy to rest on Sunday, right? Absolutely not, unless I'm intentional about doing so.

I want everything to be tidy all the time. A place for everything, and everything in its place. Basically I'm allergic to clutter. Having a toddler has relaxed me in this area, but having floors that are unswept, a full sink, and piles of laundry are three things that eat at me if they're left undone.

However, I finally decided to be "all in" and fully honor Sundays. Previously, my justification was "If I got it done before church, it didn't count as working on Sunday." Nevertheless, no more of that. I would no longer exhaust myself getting the dishes done before church and rushing to tidy up.

Saturdays are now my "get prepared for Sunday" days. Some Saturdays I get it all done; others not so much. Sometimes I get all the housework done and all laundry washed and dried but not yet folded, *and* there are still dishes in my sink.

As I mentioned before, I am still working to discipline myself in the area of resting. I admit, seeing dirty dishes on Sunday doesn't paint a smile on my face. However, I'm realizing Sunday is a day of choice. I can either wash the dishes, pout all day because they're not done, or sing praise songs to my son at breakfast while he claps his little hands.

Together, let's purposefully choose to let our minds and bodies rest by pressing the pause button on chores and errands and devoting our Sundays completely to the Lord. We've worked all week, just as God did creating the world. Let's be like-minded and take a day to rest.

Destiny K. Suarez

Thoughts and reflections:

_____

_____

_____

_____

_____

_____

Best Thing in Life:

Getting the parking spot closest to the door.

Surge Protector

Let not your heart be troubled: you believe in God,
believe also in Me.

—John 14:1

We live in an anxiety-ridden world. People are overwhelmed, fearful,
perplexed, constantly paranoid about the future, and scared of the
present.

Much of my Facebook newsfeed is flooded with anxiety memes.
When I see this, it saddens me because following the posts are
comments such as "Girl, I know; my anxiety is through the roof"
and "I totally understand the struggle. I'm a basket case."

We need not become a society that accepts anxiety as "the new
thing to have in common." Anxiety is real. It's a crippling mental
bondage but shouldn't be something that controls us. It causes one
to fret and have suspicious thoughts, to be unable to think clearly.
As a result, we overreact, shut down, or hide away in fear.

Jesus came to set us free. He knew the enemy's lies would tell us
we're inferior, incapable, and less than God created us to be. Jesus

knew how heavily this world would weigh on us and the comfort we would need, just as His disciples did.

Jesus told His disciples to not let their hearts be troubled as He tried to prepare them for His upcoming crucifixion. He let them know He would die for the sins of the world, but afterward He would be going to heaven to prepare a place for them. He painted a picture of how incredible it would be and how imperative it was for Him to go.

The next verse, John 14:2, is my favorite assurance from Jesus. He says, "If it were not so, I would have told you." Wow! The peace and comfort that are packed into this verse. Jesus is saying trust Him. He has your best interest in mind. He loves you too much to withhold any good thing from those who walk uprightly.[16] He's got you in the loop and won't lead you astray. He will never leave you alone. There's no need to fear.

When we depend upon ourselves as our only source of strength, we will quickly become overwhelmed and ultimately exhaust ourselves. In theory, it's like plugging a surge protector into its own electrical port instead of plugging it into the electrical outlet.

We cannot rely solely on ourselves to control our emotions. We must "plug in" to prayer, worship, and faith to keep our hearts and minds at rest. Submit worries and concerns to the One in whom we believe and the One who can turn our stress into peace, our fear into courage, and our inadequacy into victory.

Thoughts and reflections:

_____
_____
_____
_____
_____
_____
_____

---

[16] Psalm 84:11

Best Thing in Life:

A baby's giggle.

A Beautiful Exchange

But you have not so learned Christ, if indeed you have heard Him and have been taught by Him, as the truth is in Jesus: that you put off, concerning your former conduct, the old man which grows corrupt according to the deceitful lusts, and be renewed in the spirit of your mind, and that you put on the new man which was created according to God, in true righteousness and holiness.

—Ephesians 4:20–24

A Facebook friend posted today on her wall, "My life is falling apart, but falling together at the same time." After reading this, I felt I had been smacked in the forehead with a flashback of sorts. Several scenes played out in my head of times people walked out of my life and/or rejected me. Then I thought about the current state of my life and how I am surrounded by people who truly value and encourage me. Moments later my heart spoke, "It's been a beautiful exchange."

I was saved at seven years old, and I remember that day vividly.

I was wearing a white and tan striped shirt and khaki overall shorts. I sat in Team Kids during a Sunday night service as my pastor's wife taught a lesson. I anxiously sat in my seat because I wanted to run to the cross of the Savior I was hearing about.

During prayer time, I raised my hand to signify that I wanted to be saved. After prayer, everyone who asked Jesus into their hearts went to "big church," where we stood before the congregation, telling them we had asked Jesus into our hearts. All I remember was standing there crying, knowing I was forgiven and redeemed.

My heart overflowed with tears as I thought about the grace I had received and the love Jesus had for me. As I walked to the car after church, I looked in the goody bag my teacher had given me and pulled out a WWJD bracelet. I eagerly put it on. My mom told me, years later, that I wore that bracelet every day for a very long time, and before I would make any decision, I would look at my bracelet and ask myself, "What would Jesus do?"

At seven years old, I decided to put off the old man, or in my case the old girl, and become a new creation. Being human, I wouldn't naturally choose to do the right thing all the time. I had to be intentional about being a new creation in Christ. I knew Jesus wouldn't lie, cheat, or gossip about friends, so I had to be cautious of my thoughts and actions.

I love what Paul says in our Ephesians scripture that to be made *new* and *live a life of righteousness and holiness*, we must be *renewed in the spirit of our minds*. To be made new, we have to get rid of the old. As a friend of mine says, "We've got to get rid of that stinkin' thinkin'" by decluttering our minds and replacing how we used to think with the truth of God's Word. In doing so, formerly you would say, "I am not smart enough," but now you know God says, "I will give you wisdom."[17] When you feel all alone, He says, "I will

---

[17] 1 Corinthians 1:30

never leave you nor forsake you."[18] And when you feel you can't go on anymore, He reminds you that His grace is sufficient.[19]

When we come to Christ, we become a new creation where old things have passed away and all things become new.[20] Through reading and memorizing scripture, our minds will automatically begin to renew themselves as they dip into the reservoir of truth that fills our hearts. It will flow from our hearts to our minds and cause us to act and respond differently—to be made new.

Thoughts and reflections:

_____

_____

_____

_____

_____

_____

_____

---

[18] Hebrews 13:5
[19] 2 Corinthians 12:9
[20] 2 Corinthians 5:17

Best Thing in Life:

Driving away from the gas station with a full tank of gas.

A Chosen Path

Enter by the narrow gate; for wide is the gate and broad is the way that leads to destruction, and there are many who go in by it. Because narrow is the gate and difficult is the way which leads to life, and there are few who find it.

—Matthew 7:13–14

Robert Frost's poem, "The Road Not Taken," is one that leaped off the page when I first read it in high school, and I haven't forgotten it. It's easy to put oneself in the shoes of the traveler.

The traveler is in the woods and finds himself at a fork in the road. He chooses the road he has never traveled before. At the end, the poet says, "I took the one less traveled by, and that has made all the difference."

The closing stanza makes me think of my Christian walk. Accepting Jesus as my Savior has made all the difference for me. No matter the situation, I've had Jesus by my side, a friend that sticks closer than a brother,[21] a helper in the time of need,[22] and a refuge in the storm.[23] Truly everything I ever needed, He was and is.

Has life been peaches and ice cream, rainbows and flowers, always? Many times, far from it. I've had heartaches and trials, but I've never walked alone.

Ironically, the majority choose the road that leads to destruction. Why would anyone choose such a route? For one thing, it's easy, and the future consequences do not occur to them, only their present desires. Sadly, people also take this wide and frequently traveled road because it's popular, it's fun, and hey, who likes rules anyway?

Then there's the road that few travel. It's narrow, and it's holy. The Bible tells us *few find it*. It requires commitment to the Lord and not partaking in sin. It means praying and fasting even when you don't want to. It's choosing Him, even when no one else does.

The beauty of choosing the road that few travel is that life everlasting is your reward. After we wear out these human bodies, we get to live in heaven. There will be peace. There will be joy forever. And ultimately there will be Jesus. It's going to be a place that makes choosing the narrow path worth it.

Choose today the path you will take. Will it be destruction, or will it be life? To choose life and to choose Jesus as your Savior, you can pray this prayer below to ask Jesus into your heart:

> *Dear God, I thank You for loving me so much that You sent Your Son Jesus to die on the cross for my sins. I ask that Jesus come live in my heart. I pray You will cleanse me and forgive me for my sins. Help me to choose You each day and follow You all the days of my life. Amen.*

---

[21] Proverbs 18:24

[22] Psalm 46:1

[23] Isaiah 25:4

Thoughts and reflections:

_____

_____

_____

_____

_____

_____

_____

Destiny K. Suarez

Best Thing in Life:

Your favorite song coming on the radio.

Hear It Till You Believe It

So then faith comes by hearing, and hearing by the
word of God.

—Romans 10:17

Women don't forget what was said to them, especially by their
husbands after a heated conversation. Words have the power to take
root in our minds as we meditate on what has been spoken.

I once heard, "Your mind will believe anything you tell it." By
calling ourselves ugly, we aren't going to feel pretty and confident.
But if we tell ourselves, "You're brave. You're beautiful. You can do
anything you set your mind to," we are training our minds to believe
we are wonderful, valuable, and victorious.

The same result happens when we apply the word of God to our
lives. In the book of Romans, God has given all believers "a measure
of faith."[24] A dose of faith has been put inside us all. The first time

---

[24] Romans 12:3

we put faith into action is when we asked Jesus into our hearts. We believed He could take a sinner, forgive all their sins, make them brand new, and change their eternal destination from hell to heaven.

We heard of His love for us, how He died on the cross for our sins and is preparing a place in heaven for all who believe in Him. We recognized we were unworthy of obtaining forgiveness on our own and knew we needed a Savior. By hearing God's Word, our faith was made alive. We believed that through Jesus, we could be saved.

Feeding our minds with God's Word declutters our brains. A change takes place in how we think, the more we hear His truth. It renews our minds to the reality of who we are and who God is. Eventually our lips will speak what our heart believes.[25]

As faith increases, we believe what we cannot yet see.[26] We have hope amid fear. We walk in boldness and in the authority that Jesus walked in. After all, Jesus said greater things will be done by us than He did.[27] That's a lot of miracles and power living inside us. Our faith can cause the blind to see, the deaf to hear, the oppressed to be delivered, and the bound to be freed.

It's time to accelerate our faith. We must discipline ourselves to read and obey God's Word. It is power. It is life. It is alive! It will change our outlook on everything.

What is it you hear so much that you believe?

Thoughts and reflections:

_____

_____

_____

_____

_____

_____

_____

[25] Luke 6:45
[26] Hebrews 11:1
[27] John 14:12

Best Thing in Life:

Experiencing a pleasant scent that reminds you of your childhood.

A New Expectation

Most assuredly, I say to you, he who believes in Me, the works that I do he will do also; and greater works than these he will do, because I go to My Father. And whatever you ask in My name, that I will do, that the Father may be glorified in the Son. If you ask anything in My name, I will do it.

—John 14:12–14

Whatever you desire, expect it to come forth. Whatever you need, ask for it. Whatever you crave, seek after. Whatever was good enough last year cannot be good enough this year.

A new expectation is necessary—a new awakening, a new boldness to seek after the righteousness of our Lord. God will bring mighty things forth if we are prepared to receive and to accept what He has purposed. Jesus said we will do greater works than He did. We should expect the impossible to become possible. Divine appointments await. Chains will be broken, and victories will come from all four corners of the earth.

Great conquest waits for us. Triumph will come, but our

perseverance must be tenacious. We must be praying and fasting, with much faithfulness in serving God. The anointing will come with a price of sacrifice, but the reward will be greater.

God has promised wonderful things for His people. Our eyes cannot perceive and our minds cannot consume the majestic and awesome things He has prepared for those who know Him. It's glorious when we see His great works manifested through us. We will wink at heaven, knowing it was He who answered our prayers. We will shout and leap with joy as we see the miracles we've read about in scripture take place through us.

What miracles have you seen today?

Thoughts and reflections:

_____

_____

_____

_____

_____

_____

_____

Best Thing in Life:

The smell of summer rain.

Who Is He to You?

When Jesus came into the region of Caesarea Philippi, He asked His disciples, saying, "Who do men say that I, the Son of Man, am?"

So they said, "Some say John the Baptist, some Elijah, and others Jeremiah or one of the prophets."

He said to them, "But who do you say that I am?"

—Matthew 16:13–15

"Savior" is the first characteristic that comes to mind when I think about Jesus. However, lately, He has been revealing Himself to me as Carpenter. To identify the redeemer of the world in this way is almost strange and far from typical.

Instead, very fittingly, Jesus spent the majority of His life in His trade. For 90 percent of His life, He lived as a common man, going to work each day, something we view as the mundane.

He who would bring salvation to the world worked with His hands. He was focused on the current season instead of worrying about His next season.

Did you catch that? We try to live in the future more so than the present. We are so anxious about when we'll get the next promotion, eagerly waiting for our kids to start school, and the list goes on.

Jesus didn't spend His days worrying about if and when. His life teaches us to invest in our current season because life is but a vapor.[28] During His normal day-to-day life, He was preparing for the ministry He would begin at thirty years old. He went to the temple asking questions. He prayed to God for wisdom.

Right now, you may be wishing and waiting for a new season. You're not wrong for wanting something different or sensing the future call on your life. But instead of living discontent and engrossed by the future, meditate on your life now. How can you be used by God in your present season?

Take time to reflect on who Jesus is to you. The beauty of God is that He reveals His qualities to us more prevalently in different times of our lives. There are times when I have known Him more closely as friend, comforter, defender, rescuer, and life-giver. He has all these attributes, but now I'm knowing Him more closely as a Carpenter, not only through His earthly occupation, but as someone who is intricately concerned and purposeful in every detail of our lives.

Thoughts and reflections:

_____

_____

_____

_____

_____

_____

_____

---

[28] James 4:14

Best Thing in Life:

The fresh smell of a baby right after a bath.

Second Chance

Jesus said to her, "Neither do I condemn you; go
and sin no more."

—John 8:11b

If we were sitting around the table, and someone asked, "Who's
ever messed up?", we would all undoubtedly raise our hands. If they
followed up with, "Really bad?", we would slowly raise our hands
this time, honestly and regretfully.

There was a female in the Bible, known as "the woman caught
in adultery," who messed up and was caught in the very act.[29] If that
wasn't humiliating enough, the Pharisees brought her to Jesus at
the temple and publicly announced her sin while asking Jesus what
should be done about it. They demanded stoning her since that's
what the Law of Moses declared as punishment.

At this point in the story, I'm confident she knew she was in
the last minutes of her life. She had sinned; she was caught, and
now her consequence awaited her. I'm sure she was surprised when

---

[29] John 8:4

Jesus ignored the Pharisees and began writing in the sand. After writing, He stood up and said, "He who is without sin among you, let him throw a stone at her first."[30] If that wasn't thought-provoking enough, Jesus knelt and wrote in the sand again.

The Bible doesn't say what He wrote; I can't help but wonder if it was the names of all her accusers along with their sins. I ponder this because after Jesus wrote in the sand the second time, the Pharisees, "being convicted by their conscience, went out one by one, beginning with the oldest even to the last."[31]

All her accusers left. Those who thought she deserved death were nowhere in sight. In that moment, it was just her and Jesus. As Jesus stood up, He asked her where her accusers were and who was condemning her. She replied "No one, Lord." Jesus replied, "Neither do I condemn you. Go and sin no more."[32] The One, perfect and sinless, who had the right to judge her sin didn't. What an intimate moment she had to embrace His love and grace.

What I love about Jesus' final words to her is that He didn't say her sin was okay. He told her to not do it again. Is there anything in your life that you need to just stop doing? To stop thinking about? To stop hiding? The Bible says that we've *all* sinned and we've all fallen short.[33] But God also says, "My grace is sufficient for you, for my strength is made perfect in weakness."[34] Let's search our hearts for the messy places, repent of our sins, and with God's help go and sin no more.

---

[30] John 8:7
[31] John 8:9
[32] John 8:11
[33] Romans 3:23
[34] 2 Corinthians 12:9

Destiny K. Suarez

Thoughts and reflections:

_____

_____

_____

_____

_____

_____

_____

Best Thing in Life:

A hot shower after a long day.

If He Calls You, He's Sure

For all the promises of God in Him are Yes, and in Him Amen, to the glory of God through us. Now He who establishes us with you in Christ and has anointed us is God, who also has sealed us and given us the Spirit in our hearts as a guarantee.

—2 Corinthians 1:20–22

Have you ever felt confident in someone else's purpose more so than your own, thinking, *They're so good at what they do—a complete natural, confident, eloquent in speech—and outwardly they have it all together, and I don't?*

It's silly how our minds go to places of disappointment for not being someone else. This goes way back to elementary school when we were picked last to be on a team, or we were humiliated for missing an easy word during a spelling bee, or we couldn't run on the treadmill at the gym like the other girls.

We see strength in others but question our own abilities, convinced we're not good, smart, talented, or brave enough to have a significant purpose in the kingdom of God.

I found myself in this exact place recently. God revealed to me that I was called to evangelize. I had led different classes in church before, sung in church, and loved traveling, but when God spoke this to me, it gave me, in Southern terms, the heebie-jeebies.

I grew up in church revivals and saw the great ministers of God. They spoke with power and authority revealing they were "made for this." But me? Was I called to do this too? I became nervous because I didn't have business cards or connections to get speaking engagements.

A few days after God spoke, my heart reminded me if this was what I was going to do, then God had the puzzle pieces already put together. His words are "yes" and "amen." They are true, they are steadfast, and they are secure.

My heart took refuge in realizing that God already knew the churches, the dates, and all the arrangements. I didn't have to worry about the details. I just had to be obedient.

So I prayed to God, "Here am I," just as Isaiah answered God. I told Him I would go and do whatever He wanted me to do. I asked God to make me like Ezekiel and let my lips only speak the words He wanted to come out of my mouth when opportunities came.

Within a few days, I was asked to preach at my home church, to sing at a church revival, and then to speak at a women's conference. Go, God! He was faithful to His call.

I tell you this story because God has a purpose for your life too. Before God created the world, He chose us.[35] He already had a plan that would unfold in our lives if we would accept His will.

Even if you have to do it afraid, reach out and grab hold of your purpose today. Tell God you want all that He has in store for you. Trust that He is all-knowing and holds promises for you that are

---

[35] Ephesians 1:4

good. You are fully capable, and no one else in this world can be the you God called you to be.

Thoughts and reflections:

_____
_____
_____
_____
_____
_____
_____

Best Thing in Life:

A warm embrace.

Weathered from the Storm

Hear my cry, O God; attend unto my prayer.
From the end of the earth will I cry unto thee, when
my heart is overwhelmed: lead me to the rock that
is higher than I.
For thou hast been a shelter for me, and a strong
tower from the enemy.

—Psalm 61:1–3

No one likes to go out in the rain, especially us women, particularly on the days we have a good hair day and we see the bottom has fallen out of the sky. To make matters worse, our umbrella is in the car.

Rain mixed with wind, lightning, and thunder can cause fear. As we watch trees bending, leaves flying in the air, lightning eerily flashing in the dark sky, and hear thunder booming, we become anxious about when it will end, scared of the destruction it may bring.

Several storms in the Bible occurred while Jesus and His disciples were at sea. Once, after they had fed five thousand men with just five loaves of bread and two fish,[36] Jesus told them to get in a boat and head to Bethsaida while He sent the multitude away. Once they got to the middle of the sea, they began struggling to row the boat as the wind blew harshly.

Jesus could see them struggling[37] to remain in control of the boat as He stood on top of the mountain where He had gone to pray. Jesus went down to the sea and began to walk on the water. The Bible said He would have walked right passed His disciples had they not yelled out to Him, fearful He was a ghost. Jesus responded, "Be of good cheer! It is I; do not be afraid."[38]

Jesus was, miraculously, walking on the water *while* having a conversation with the disciples. He was walking on the very thing troubling His disciples, the waves. They had rowed and rowed against violent waves, trying so hard to keep control of their boat. Jesus walked on the same waves as if He were taking a stroll in the park. He was calm, peaceful, and in control. The Bible then tells us that as soon as He entered the boat with the disciples, the winds ceased.[39]

This story made me not only think of the physical storms outside, but also the storms in our personal lives. Situations like getting a call that brings devastating news, finding out our pipes are now leaking in the house, or not having enough money coming in to pay all the bills that are due. What if we'd invite Jesus into our boat, our lives?

He is all-knowing. Just as He saw the disciples in the middle of the sea, He has His eyes on you and me too. At all times, He knows exactly where we are and what we are facing. We don't have to row our boat alone and be battered by life's waves.

Jesus tells us to cast all our cares on Him, because He cares for

---

[36] Mark 6:30–44
[37] Mark 6:48
[38] Mark 6:50
[39] Mark 6:51

Destiny K. Suarez

us.[40] When we pray to Him about what we have going on in our lives, He will come get in our boat. He will give us His peace that surpasses all understanding.[41] Not only that, our prayers of faith will change our circumstances.

Just as Jesus fed thousands of people with one little boy's lunch, He can take whatever we have and create hope and abundance. We must include Him and trust that He is in control; His plans for us are good.[42]

Thoughts and reflections:

_____

_____

_____

_____

_____

_____

_____

---

[40] 1 Peter 5:7
[41] Philippians 4:7
[42] Jeremiah 29:11

Best Thing in Life:

Experiencing warm heat after being in the frigid cold.

Final Round

I want you to be wise in what is good, and simple concerning evil. And the God of peace will crush Satan under your feet shortly.

—Romans 16:19–20

Good and evil have been at war since the beginning of time. God created the earth, as related in the first chapter of Genesis; by chapter 3 the fall of man had happened, and sin entered the world.

Satan had convinced Eve that the tree God told them they couldn't eat from, really, they could. He twisted God's command to trick Eve into committing the first sin. Eve fell into his sly persuasion. Then she convinced Adam to sin too by telling him how yummy the fruit from the forbidden tree was.

Lying, stealing, and destroying are still the traits of Satan, our enemy. He is a pro at causing deception, confusion, and ruin. He wants everything opposed to what God wants for His creation.

Sin separates us from God because He is holy and righteous. In the Old Testament, sacrifices were the only way for sins to be forgiven. There were lots of regulations on how a sacrifice was to properly be conducted.

The New Testament brought the ultimate sacrifice. God sent His only Son, Jesus, born of a virgin, to bring salvation to the world. He lived sinless His entire thirty-three years on the earth. Although perfect and not needing repentance Himself, He took the place of the sacrificial animal used formerly in the Old Testament. He was the only sacrifice God would accept to forgive all the sins of mankind.

He was beaten until He was unrecognizable. His beard was plucked from His face, and a crown of thorns was placed on His head, as many mocked Him. He was nailed to a wooden cross and died for you and me.

I'm in utter awe of how much He loves us, so much that we were worth all the pain He endured. His love and willingness to die for us paid our debt to erase our sins, past, present, and future.

The final victory wasn't in His death, though. Three days after He was buried in a borrowed tomb, He was resurrected from the dead. Even death had no hold on Him.

Jesus gives us the same authority that He has when we ask Him to come into our hearts and forgive us of our sins. He gives us His Holy Spirit, that will be a comforter to us and a discerner of good and evil.

The Bible tells us to resist the devil and he will flee.[43] God will strengthen us and help us make wise choices even when we're tempted to sin. The devil is roaming throughout the earth, like a lion, seeking who he may devour because he knows his time left on earth is short.[44] On the contrary, the Lord also goes to and fro throughout the whole earth, to show Himself strong on behalf of those whose hearts are loyal to Him.[45]

---

[43] James 4:7
[44] 1 Peter 5:8
[45] 2 Chronicles 16:9

Destiny K. Suarez

Satan's freedom to cause calamity won't be forever. As believers in Christ, we can rest in the truth that the end has already been written. We win. Satan will be locked up for eternity in hell. Jesus conquered the grave to give us eternal life, and with Jesus as our focus, we have heaven to gain.

We must have the truth of God's Word in our hearts and minds to quickly be able to acknowledge the enemy's schemes. How will you fight the good fight and choose what is righteous and holy?

Thoughts and reflections:

_____

_____

_____

_____

_____

_____

_____

Best Thing in Life:

First sip of a canned soda.

What's Most Important?

All Scripture is given by inspiration of God, and is profitable for doctrine, for reproof, for correction, for instruction in righteousness, that the man of God may be complete, thoroughly equipped for every good work.

—2 Timothy 3:16–17

Do you ever feel overwhelmed? Do this, do that. Not that way, this way. Dinner needs to have two healthy vegetables, and not more than one of them can be a starch. Also, make sure it's dairy-free and gluten-free. Don't forget to wash the uniforms for tomorrow night's game. Your brother's birthday party is Friday at two p.m., and it's very important that you're there. Don't hold your babies too long, or you're going to spoil them. Make sure you give to the building fund and youth fundraiser, make something for the bake sale, and sign up to volunteer in youth group at least twice quarterly.

Even though this list has good things, it can be exhausting and honestly makes me feel like I can never do enough. I love serving, being a hostess, and taking care of my family, but does having the longest list or being signed up the most often make me worth any more?

Instead, it leaves me tired, because Grandma told me I should make it a priority and my coworker suggested it'd be a great fit. My brain feels so overloaded. I need to be this and don't forget to do that. I'm drained and feel like a failure.

One day while I was walking at the park, a thought came to me: what does God say is most important? The Bible is full of wisdom, guidance, and truth. I felt like I needed God to simplify my life. My plate was too full, and I didn't like not measuring up. I wasn't sinning, but I sure didn't have the joy the Bible talks about. I felt more like a rat running a race.

As I was walking and listening to my audible, I heard the story of the scribes asking Jesus what the greatest commandment was. Jesus replied with two commandments. He said, "'You shall love the Lord your God with all your heart, with all your soul, and with all your mind.' This is the first and great commandment. And the second is like it: 'You shall love your neighbor as yourself.' On these two commandments hang all the Law and the Prophets."[46] Out of everything we do, it all boils down to the question of whether God is first in our lives and whether we're loving people well.

Suddenly "doing all I can" had a new meaning. This revelation chopped my to-do list in half, and every suggestion of what I *should* do vanished. None of that mattered anymore.

I did a self-evaluation. After all, I wasn't going to give an account to Sister Susie or anyone else. That conversation would be with God. Ultimately, all He wants is to be first in my life. Meaning, I need to make time each day to talk to Him and read His Word.

Second, am I loving others as I should be? Not just how I think they should be loved, but treating them as I would myself, speaking with kindness, giving a smile or hug, and letting them know I value them.

---

[46] Matthew 22:37–40

Then, after I've done those two things, everything else will follow without guilt. Yes, the day-to-day duties will still be there. But I won't be a basket case because I will have spent time with the Lord refreshing my soul, and I'll know I helped others bloom as I watered them with my love. I will be better balanced if I continue to value God's two commandments in the same order He does.

Thoughts and reflections:

_____

_____

_____

_____

_____

_____

_____

Best Thing in Life:

An empty sink or clothes basket (even if it's for five minutes).

Secret Sin

> But the Comforter, which is the Holy Ghost, whom the Father will send in my name, he shall teach you all things, and bring all things to your remembrance, whatsoever I have said unto you.
>
> —John 14:26

Yesterday my husband and I had the chance to lie. The kind of lie you tell when you know the truth won't help you. Sometimes it's referred to as "fudging a little."

The little voice in my head said, *No one will know.* And it was right ... no one except for God, my husband, and myself. I know you've been there before, right? Knowing how to make the game plan work, especially if you don't play exactly by the rules.

Earlier in the day, I had skipped my workout to spend time with God. I woke up with my soul feeling dry. As I prayed, I told God what we needed, reminded Him of His promises, and told Him I trusted Him. Later in the afternoon, my husband and I went to see the person who would be the decider of our "fate." She would tell us yes or no.

Before going inside, we sat in the car analyzing our situation, knowing what would give us a yes, but also knowing what was on paper screamed no. We decided to hush our voices and pray silently. The interviewer began with basic questions where the truth was easy: "What is your name?" Check, got that one right. Then came the hard questions, to me first, along with the opportunity to fudge half the truth—well, honestly, any "truth" I wanted to give. I sat there in silence for what felt like eternity until my lips spoke the truth. The crazy thing is it wasn't me that spoke but the Holy Spirit speaking through me.

Next, it was my husband's turn. I was so proud of him. He didn't skip a beat in answering truthfully. I sat there thinking, *Well it's out there. The truth. The truth that looks like scribbles on paper. The truth that gets our request denied.*

Let me pause for a moment and say, "Lord, forgive me for any time I have judged someone for a selfish decision they made—for example, Abraham. God told him he would have generations of children, but he got tired of waiting and took matters into his own hands. He believed God's promise, but he also knew how to guarantee what he wanted. He knew how to make it happen on his own. And boy, so did I yesterday."

We've all been tempted and almost did the wrong thing or actually did it. To finish my story, the representative told us she would call the next day. When I got back to the car, I felt a weight lifted. It felt really good to have a clear conscience.

Less than an hour after the business opened, she called me and said, "Mrs. Suarez, everything has been approved." After doing a praise dance in my kitchen, I immediately thought, *Isn't that just like God? What was a rejection on paper couldn't be denied by His goodness and faithfulness.*

When we spend time with God, the Holy Spirit will steer us to walk uprightly. As sheep we naturally want to run off, so we need our Shepherd to keep us close to Him.[47] He will keep us in line.

I encourage you to do the hard things, to stand for truth. Choose righteousness over selfish ambition because blessed are those who walk according to God's law.[48]

He's good. He's faithful. And His promises are true. Don't settle for half by taking matters into your own hands. Trust Him to provide the whole.

Thoughts and reflections:

_____

_____

_____

_____

_____

_____

_____

---

[47] Psalm 23:1–6
[48] Psalm 119:1

Best Thing in Life:

Watching your alma mater team play at a sporting event.

Match Gone Missing

As it is written,
"Eye has not seen,
Nor ear heard,
Nor have entered into the heart of man,
The things which God has prepared for those who
love Him."

—1 Corinthians 2:9

While folding multiple loads of laundry, I saved the socks for last. Every sock had a match except for one of my black socks. My shoulders drooped as I told myself, *The dryer really does eat socks.*

As I was putting the paired socks away, I dropped the single sock to the side. It was then that I noticed there was another single black sock lying at the edge of the drawer. I was giddy that I had found its match. Upon pairing and folding the two socks, I had an epiphany: What if what we see isn't all that's there? Perhaps what we long for is already available; we just haven't seen it yet.

Like the hidden sock, the Bible tells us no eye has seen all that God has for those who love Him. We can't even fathom the blessings and plans He has in store. It's all beyond our imagination, incredibly indescribable. Yet, it's already purposed and available to those who draw close to Him.

The mysterious wonders of God will be revealed to those who seek Him.[49] There's no doubt that when we seek after God, we will find Him.[50] Even though we cannot physically see Him, His Word tells us He's not far from us at all.[51]

Just as you would call a friend to share exciting news or ask for advice, you can pause to talk to God. The big and the small are important to Him. Isn't it amazing that the Creator of the entire universe desires to have an intimate relationship with us? He created us for that very purpose. He sent Jesus to die for our sins so that we could be forgiven and live for eternity with Him in heaven.

We are His children. He also calls us His friends when we forsake the ways of the world and cleave to His commandments. When we obey God's laws, we are expressing our covenant with Him. We show our love to Him by our faithfulness and obedience.

David wrote in Psalm 63 how he thirsted for God as one would thirst for water in a desert. He craved time with God. He longed deeply for relationship with the Father, just as we should. You may ask, How do I do that? The Bible says to seek Him with our whole heart, to hold nothing back, and to come to Him in complete surrender and commitment, desiring to know Him more.

To know Him is to know His Word. To read and study the Bible is to know who God is and discover the treasures that He has for His children. How vast, how wide, and how deep is the love of God for us—the immeasurable gifts He has in store for those who diligently seek them.

---

[49] 1 Corinthians 2:10
[50] Jeremiah 29:13
[51] Acts 17:27

Thoughts and reflections:

_____

_____

_____

_____

_____

_____

_____

Best Thing in Life:

Beginning a new book.

From Manger to Throne

Jesus answered, "Most assuredly, I say to you, unless
one is born of water and the Spirit, he cannot enter
the kingdom of God."

—John 3:5

Smelly animals and dirty floors: no one would one enjoy this, much
less desire to birth a baby in it. However, this was the setting in
which Mary birthed the Son of God.

On the contrary, it could've been Jerusalem's version of a five-
star hotel, with many servants pampering Mary as she gave birth,
including luxury incense that filled the room and created a calm
ambience. As soon as Jesus was born, a jeweled crown would be
placed on His head, proclaiming His title as the chosen Messiah.

But none of that was the case. Neither a private birthing room
nor a calm nursery was available—only a stable filled with animals
and a feeding trough in which to lay Baby Jesus.

God's plan was for Jesus to be born in a lowly environment,
atypical for a king. From the very beginning, and in the prophecies

of Jesus' birth, God had already established the location, time, and arrangements as to how His Son would arrive.

I find it humbling that God would bring the Savior of the world to the earth to be born in such a simple way. It shows how little God is concerned with the material things of this world, yet how deeply passionate He is about spiritual things.

We might have all the luxurious automobiles, elaborate homes, designer bags, fancy electronics, and exotic vacations but still lack if we're not careful. God is solely focused on what our heart possesses. First, and above all, does it include Him? Unless we have made Jesus our Lord, all we have are earthly riches that will one day pass away.

The Bible tells us to not store our treasures here on earth, where moth and rust will corrupt them and thieves take hold of them. These earthly riches are mere dust, but spiritual things will never lose their value. Therefore, God tells us to lay up our treasures in heaven where they'll last and be safe forever.[52] When we choose Jesus, we have an everlasting kingdom to gain.

Jesus' first home in the world, a stable filled with hay, is no longer where He lives. His royal throne is positioned at the right hand of God, and many crowns are placed continually at His feet by believers who are in heaven with Him.[53]

We have this same heaven to gain, dear sisters. Let's not worry about keeping up with the Joneses or measuring ourselves by social media's depiction of what we should have, be, or do. Let's concentrate on having more spiritual treasures and leaving a legacy of eternal impact for the kingdom of God.

---

[52] Mathew 6:19–20 (KJV)
[53] Revelation 4:10 (KJV)

Thoughts and reflections:

_____

_____

_____

_____

_____

_____

Best Thing in Life:

The taste of a chocolate bar melting in your mouth.

When Everything I Do Gets Undone

Then the King will say to those on His right hand, "Come, you blessed of My Father, inherit the kingdom prepared for you from the foundation of the world: for I was hungry and you gave Me food; I was thirsty and you gave Me drink; I was a stranger and you took Me in; I was naked and you clothed Me; I was sick and you visited Me; I was in prison and you came to Me."

Then the righteous will answer Him, saying, "Lord, when did we see You hungry and feed You, or thirsty and give You drink? When did we see You a stranger and take You in, or naked and clothe You? Or when did we see You sick, or in prison, and come to You?" And the King will answer and say to them, "Assuredly, I say to you, inasmuch as you did it to one of the least of these My brethren, you did it to Me."

—Matthew 25:34–40

I pick up the toys off the floor and place them in the toy bin. Fold the blankets that are tossed on the couch and wipe off the end tables with glass cleaner to remove all the fingerprints.

Within minutes, the toys are once again scattered on the floor, even more than those I picked up the first time. The blankets have become ghost costumes. The only evidence of a little human underneath is the glimpse of small feet scurrying around the room as he laughs with glee. "Uh-oh," I hear, as my heart sinks, wondering if he has spilled his milk—again.

Finally, with at least the dishes done, I go in the living room only to find an empty bowl from last night's ice cream snack. Does the sink ever stay empty longer than thirty seconds?

Do you ever feel like everything you do gets undone? I find myself in this place quite often. The desire for my home to look like the feature in a home and garden magazine is something I have to daily surrender.

During my morning Bible reading, I stumbled across the verse, "Whatever you do, do it heartily, as to the Lord and not to men, knowing that from the Lord you will receive the reward of the inheritance; for you serve the Lord Christ."[54] My heart filled with repentance, surrender, and sudden eagerness to do another task.

My thoughts went from *Oh, I have to do this, and this, and so on* to *I get to do this and this, for God.*

Do I now enjoy doing dishes? No. It's my least favorite chore, but it shifts my thoughts from becoming bitter and frustrated to recognizing I get to perform an honorable act of service to God, not to mention appreciating that I have dishes to wash, which means I have plenty of food to eat … and so on.

It truly goes back to renewing our minds with the truth. When we feel we *have* to do something, it's easy to feel unappreciated and wonder if what we do really matters. But if we considered the things we do daily, even chores, as doing them for the Lord, our attitude will change.

---

[54] Colossians 3:23–24

Will we get it right all the time? Probably not. But quite possibly, we will start a revival in our homes. As the saying goes, "If Mama ain't happy, ain't nobody happy." We can choose to be women of joy because we have our minds set toward serving the King. After all, we're called to be helpmates to our husbands, and we're raising children to be in God's army. Additionally, we're called to be servants of Christ.

No task at hand is small, but the reward is eternally worth it.

Thoughts and reflections:

_____

_____

_____

_____

_____

_____

_____

Best Thing in Life:

Refreshing taste of ice water after a long walk.

You're Just Fine

And my God shall supply all your need according
to His riches in glory by Christ Jesus.
—Philippians 4:19

As I stood at the sink washing dishes, my son sat at the table nearby
with his cereal, his spoon, and a cup of juice. Nevertheless, he
shouted toward me, "Ehhhh. Ehhhh."

I turned around to look at him and said, "Baby, you're just fine.
You have everything you need." I dropped the dishrag into the sink
as I felt God speaking the same phrase to me: *Daughter, you're just
fine. You have everything you need.*

I placed my hands on the edge of the sink and whispered, "God,
I trust you."

My husband hit a deer in the early hours of the morning,
several days before Christmas, and we recently received the news
that there was a 99 percent chance our car would be deemed a
total loss. Not to mention that two days before the accident, we
met with our Realtor and mortgage broker to discuss purchasing
a new home.

It felt as though our dreams were taking a turn, a bad one at that. Instead of using the money we'd saved for a down payment on a house, we would now be paying an insurance deductible or purchasing another car with a new loan.

I racked my brain for several days about our dilemma and how we would navigate it while wishing I could just make it all go away. God knew I needed a reminder that He already had everything figured out. We weren't *going to be just fine*. We already *were just fine*.

Just as my son thought I might have forgotten something, we often feel that way about God. Looking at social media can make us feel as though we aren't measuring up, as though we don't have *something* that everyone else seems to have, as though we're always having to resort to plan B.

Yet all the while, God reminds us we're just fine and have everything we need. God isn't burdened by our dilemmas, and He isn't anxious about the outcome. He knows the storms, trials, and setbacks before they happen. He's prepared and already knows what we need. He owns it all and can supply it all.

So why do we stumble in our faith and think that God won't provide? He already gave us the greatest gift, His Son, to die for our sins. Furthermore, He promises to not hold back any other good gift from those who walk uprightly.[55]

Instead of doubting and being fearful of all the what-ifs, let's come to Him as little children, crying out to our Father and taking everything to Him in prayer.[56] When we ask Him for what we need, it will be given to us. When we look for Him, we will find Him.[57] He will attend to our cries, meet our needs, and fulfill His promises as a good Father.[58]

---

[55] Psalm 84:11 (KJV)
[56] Philippians 4:6 (KJV)
[57] Luke 11:9 (KJV)
[58] Matthew 7:11 (KJV)

Thoughts and reflections:

_____

_____

_____

_____

_____

_____

Best Thing in Life:

Hearing "I love you."

Either I Believe God or I Don't

If any of you lacks wisdom, let him ask of God, who gives to all liberally and without reproach, and it will be given to him. But let him ask in faith, with no doubting, for he who doubts is like a wave of the sea driven and tossed by the wind. For let not that man suppose that he will receive anything from the Lord; he is a double-minded man, unstable in all his ways.

—James 1:5–8

As the saying goes, "When the rubber meets the road, we find out what we're made of." We find out if we're stable and rooted or weak and faint of heart. Do we panic and bite our fingernails when we don't see a solution to our problem, or do we remain steadfast in our faith that God will provide?

My husband hit a deer five days before Christmas. His position at work was eliminated two days before New Year's Eve, and on January 2, we were told our car was totaled from the car accident.

I had a come-to-Jesus meeting with a friend of mine, the day after my husband lost his job. I told her, "Either I believe God or I don't. I can't just pick and choose when I will trust Him." As I spoke these words, I was affirmed within myself where my roots were. I had immersed myself in the Bible the whole year prior, reading it from cover to cover.

Some might question, "You were so faithful to God. Why has He let these things happen to you?" I didn't have time to let those questions set up camp in my mind. I knew who I believed in. Many times over, He has been faithful to me just as the psalmist David wrote, "I have been young, and now am old; yet I have not seen the righteous forsaken, nor his descendants begging bread."[59]

God didn't forget me when my grandma passed away and I trekked from South Carolina to Texas to pack up her home and bring her cremated ashes back. He provided when we were about to lose our house in the first year of our marriage. We were two months behind on our rent because of a job loss, and when we called our landlord to let him know we wouldn't be able to afford to live there anymore, not only did he forgive the two months' debt, he also promised to reduce our rent by a hundred dollars each month for the next year.

God brought my son into this world safely after I'd been induced for nearly three days. The doctors didn't understand why I had only dilated halfway, but when he was born via C-section, we learned that his head was tilted on my pelvic bone. Had I birthed him naturally, his neck would have broken as he came through the birthing canal.

I believe there is a God who is working everything for my good and who has angels fighting on my behalf. He is right there with you, too.

The Bible tells us, whatever we lack, to ask Him for it. Our endless questions don't burden Him one bit. It's impossible for us to overwhelm Him. In Him, there is no lack.

---

[59] Psalm 37:25

We must make our minds up to be rooted in Him, not to be tossed around like the waves in the sea when uncertain situations arise. Scripture tells us those who doubt shouldn't expect anything from God. I don't want that to be me, and I can bet you're shaking your head and don't want that for yourself either.

I say with confidence that we desire to live in the abundance of God. We want to live in His blessings, standing in awe of His faithfulness. Let's anchor our faith in God's truth and boldly make this faith-filled declaration today: Either I believe Him or I don't.

Thoughts and reflections:

_____

_____

_____

_____

_____

_____

_____

Best Thing in Life:

Getting a card in the mail from a loved one.

The Finish Line Is Ahead

I have fought the good fight, I have finished the race, I have kept the faith. Finally, there is laid up for me the crown of righteousness, which the Lord, the righteous Judge, will give to me on that Day, and not to me only but also to all who have loved His appearing.

—2 Timothy 4:7–8

Several years ago, I added "sign up for a 5K race" to my bucket list. Did I like to run? Nope. Did I enjoy exercise? Absolutely not. I couldn't understand why people woke up at four a.m. to run miles before going to work. Those people couldn't possibly be normal.

Just a little over a year ago, I had a reality check that I needed to get healthy after seeing a family photo taken on Thanksgiving. Negative feelings about myself played in my mind as I stared at the photo. I couldn't believe that was me.

Ever since middle school, I have yo-yoed on the scale. Unfortunately, the scale went up more than it went down. If I lost twenty pounds, I would only keep it off for a couple of months and then eventually gain it back, plus five or ten pounds.

After reflecting on this painful truth, I was ready for a change that would last. I began a healthy lifestyle, and the numbers on the scale began to get smaller and smaller. I knew I didn't want to have loose skin from losing a lot of weight, so joining the gym was a must. I needed to tone and become more active.

I was excited about our gym membership until it came to the working-out part. The treadmill was a drag. One tenth of a mile felt as if I had walked for an hour.

One day, one of the gym employees asked me if I had walked the track behind the gym. I told her no; however, I was eager to try after she told me many prayers had been prayed over that track.

During my first lap, the wind blew calmly, and the scenery was stunning, so I decided to do two laps, which equaled one mile. I did it. On my drive home, I remembered one thing on my bucket was to complete a 5K race. What better place to train than a track surrounded by gorgeous green grass, tranquility, and signs with motivational quotes around every turn?

Each week I added a half a mile to my walk, and in less than a month, I was able to walk three miles—enough to complete a 5K! I was thrilled to have reached this goal, but I'll tell you that last lap whooped me. The hill was tall, and my legs were burning. I didn't think I would finish.

As I was struggling, I thought, *The end of this lap is just ahead. I can't stop now.* As I continued walking, I began to think about this in a spiritual sense. Once we are saved, we begin a race that will continue for the rest of our lives. Throughout this race, there will be seasons where we are making wonderful strides. We are strong and full of energy. But along this race, there will be disappointments, setbacks, and hurdles. We cannot quit despite these hardships.

Serving the Lord isn't a "when I feel like it" or "when I have the energy" kind of decision. We must stay focused and continue to train spiritually so that we can complete our race. This training takes place when we pray to God for wisdom, read our Bible to know Him more, and attend church services surrounded by fellow believers.

While we run our race, we have the confidence of knowing that Jesus is the finisher of our faith.[60] Just as He won His race, conquering sin and the grave, He will help us win ours. We'll take on His endurance to finish by walking in the way of the Lord and seeking Him with our whole hearts.[61]

If we faint not, we will receive the ultimate prize at the end, which is eternal life. Fighting the good fight of faith, to complete our race, will reward us with a life spent with Jesus forever.

Thoughts and reflections:

_____

_____

_____

_____

_____

_____

_____

---

[60] Hebrews 12:2–3 KJV
[61] Psalm 119:1–2

Best Thing in Life:

Finding something you thought you'd lost.

Light in the Distance

But you are a chosen generation, a royal priesthood,
a holy nation, His own special people, that you may
proclaim the praises of Him who called you out of
darkness into His marvelous light.

—1 Peter 2:9

Lighthouses are invaluable for ships when sailing. The tall tower has
a bright light that serves to warn of dangerous waters or hazardous
shoals and as a navigational aid to captains and sailors.

Jesus calls us the light of the world.[62] We are to shine bright and
be separate from the world.[63] The only way to do so is by intimately
knowing the creator of light, who is God. Once we do, this is how
our story will be written:

> She saw a light. It was bright and captivating,
> enabling her to find true identity. It wasn't in the
> clothes she wore, the makeup that hid her flaws, or

---

[62] Matthew 5:14 (KJV)
[63] 2 Corinthians 6:17 (KJV)

the achievements on the wall. It was found in a love letter written thousands of years ago.

She was chosen with a purpose and with a call that would change the world. She planted her feet and couldn't be shaken, because she knew who had made her His child. He says she is wonderfully made, and because of that, she chooses to believe it for herself.

God took away the sin that made her dirty, insecure, and ashamed. His Son's blood on the cross set her free, and she was forgiven. So she picked up her purpose and straightened her crown. She inherited royalty and is now a princess.

She shows the world what it is like to be loved and cherished. She praises the Lord for His goodness upon her life and shares Christ's love to everyone she meets.

This girl is you. Shine your light so bright that all may see your good deeds and glorify God.[64]

Thoughts and reflections:

_____

_____

_____

_____

_____

_____

_____

---

[64] Matthew 5:16 (KJV)

Best Thing in Life:

Finding a $5 bill in your coat pocket.

Pursued and Purposed

For by him were all things created, that are in heaven, and that are in earth, visible and invisible, whether they be thrones, or dominions, or principalities, or powers: all things were created by him, and for him: and he is before all things, and by him all things consist.

—Colossians 1:16–17 (KJV)

My hips are too wide. My chin is too pointy. My arms sag. I only own three pairs of shoes: tennis shoes, flip-flops, and old boots. My hair needs a trim, and while we're at it, add some color to cover up that gray.

"When I become this, or I accomplish that, then I will be _____." We plan our successes based on our idea of "if" and "when," as though certain things must happen to define our purpose.

One of my favorite things about God is that we don't have to create what He's already purposed. Before we were formed in the womb,[65] God knew us. Thousands of generations before our parents were born, God already knew they would conceive you and me. Not only that, God said He *knew* us, meaning we were fully known by Him.

He knew all our talents, all our mishaps, what makes our temper flare, exactly how we like our coffee, or how sweet we like our tea. He knew what makes our hearts swoon, what causes us regret, and what would be our greatest joys.

The beauty of God knowing us is that we're His creation, and He doesn't create anything without assigning it a purpose. You may feel hesitant to believe this because of your past, body image, or how others have viewed you. But truthfully, God knew all you would do, say, and think the instant He had His first thought in creating you.

Thankfully, we do not have to align with what the world calls popular. After all, David was appointed king after tending smelly sheep. When Samuel arrived at Jesse's house, the place the Lord had sent him to anoint the next king, he had his sights on who he thought would be king as soon as he saw Jesse's oldest son. He was attractive, tall, and altogether outwardly perfect to be king.[66] But in the same moment, the Lord rebuked Samuel. He reminded him that God doesn't qualify someone based on their outward appearance but instead looks at the heart.

After Jesse's sons stood before Samuel, Samuel knew the Lord hadn't appointed any of them to be king, so He asked Jesse if all his sons were present. Jesse replied that there was one more.

Talk about being forgotten. Here the prophet is coming to your house to announce who will be the next king, and you invite only the best-looking, of excellent stature, and "guaranteed to be picked" sons to come to dinner with Samuel.

David was forgotten—or better stated, left out. He didn't get to

---

[65] Jeremiah 1:5
[66] 1 Samuel 16:6–7

take the day off to meet the prophet, getting the chance to become king. He had to continue his day job of tending sheep.

However, what God has purposed we don't have to create on our own, nor can we be denied what is already purposed to be ours. So Samuel told Jesse to send for David, and he would wait for him. Immediately, when Samuel laid eyes on the ruddy boy, the Lord spoke to him, saying, "Arise, anoint him; for this is the one!"[67]

You're also the one! God has chosen you for positions, placements, territories, and assignments that have your name already on them. You don't have to hope you qualify for what God has for you. He's already purposed for you to possess it.

He created everything for His glory, and beautiful friend, that includes you.

Thoughts and reflections:

_____

_____

_____

_____

_____

_____

_____

---

[67] 1 Samuel 16:12

Best Thing in Life:

The relief of having someone scratch your
back in a place you couldn't reach.

A Note from Destiny

I hope you finish this book feeling refreshed, chosen, loved, and adored. Let your joy radiate like the sun.

As a daughter of the King of kings, may you walk in your purpose, reclaim your thoughts, and know that you are not alone in this world. You have a mighty purpose. Princess, you've been handpicked by the King.

—Destiny

Let's Connect!

Connect with Destiny for daily inspiration and biblical encouragement and to follow her speaking schedule.

Blog: <u>www.seeingthroughtheeyesofgrace.wordpress.com</u>
Facebook: <u>www.facebook.com/destinyksuarez</u>